D0990220

EARTH ALIVE!

FOR JOSEPH AND ANNIE,
two very special earth explorers.
Your North Carolina mountain home
is one of my favorite places on earth.

I would like to thank Dr. Gerald H. Krockover,
Professor of Earth and Atmospheric Science Education
at Purdue University, for sharing his valuable expertise.
S.M.

PHOTO CREDITS
Courtesy Ward's Natural Science Establishment Inc.: pp. 2–3, 4, 7, 8, 13, 14, 22, 26, 29, 33, 35, 39. Courtesy U. S. Geological Survey Photographic Library, U. S. Department of the Interior: 6, 11, 12 (both), 23 (both), 24, 36, 38. Courtesy The Smithsonian Institution: 16 (Photo No. 89-6529), 17 (Photo Nos. 87-6408 & 77-10629), 18 (Photo Nos. 77-10594 & 78-9902). Courtesy U. S. Department of Agriculture: 31. Courtesy National Park Service, Yosemite National Park: 20. Courtesy Laura Goldsmith: 25. Galen Rowell/Mountain Light Photography: 1, 27, 30, 37. Kim Heacox/ Earth Images: 28. V. Henry/Taurus Photos, Inc. : 10.

Library of Congress Cataloging in Publication Data Markle, Sandra. Earth alive! / by Sandra Markle. p. cm. Includes bibliographical references. Summary: Describes the ways in which the earth is constantly changing and examines the reasons for and the effects of these changes. ISBN 0-688-09360-4.—ISBN 0-688-09361-2 (lib. bdg.) 1. Earth sciences—Juvenile literature. [1. Earth sciences.] I. Title. QE29.M25   1990 550—dc20 90-5803 CIP AC

EARTH ALIVE!

SANDRA MARKLE

LOTHROP, LEE & SHEPARD BOOKS NEW YORK

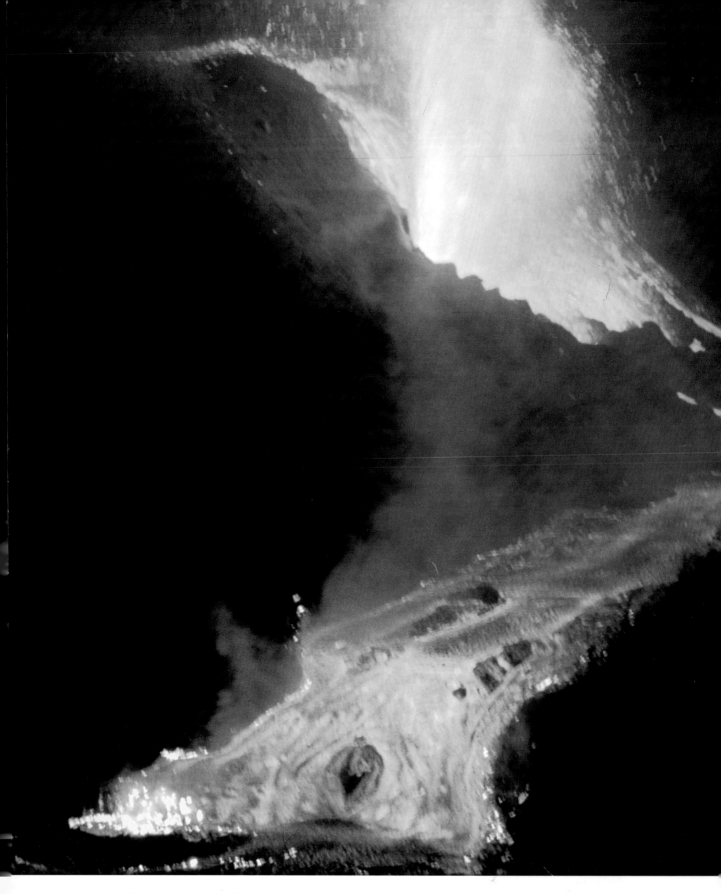

The Hawaiian Islands are famous for their active volcanoes, such as this one at Kilauea Iki.

IMAGINE your neighborhood on a Monday morning. What do you see? your mom or dad fixing breakfast? your cat scratching at the window to get in? trees blowing in the wind? What do you hear? a baby crying? dogs barking at the mailman? birds chirping on branches? Is the weather cold and windy? hot and dry? raining cats and dogs?

Everything seems to be doing something or making some sound—everything but the earth itself. Our planet seems to be doing nothing at all. But scientists know that the earth does change. Deep below us cauldrons of steam and melted rock bubble and boil. Flowing waters at the surface carry bits and pieces of earth and plants from place to place. Sometimes the ground even splits open in an earthquake.

It usually takes centuries, hundreds and thousands of them, for changes in our planet to happen. But there are some places where we can see what an active, constantly changing world the earth really is. This book will show you a few of these amazing places. There are many others that you can search out for yourself.

WINTER PARK, Florida, didn't always have a swimming hole smack dab in the middle of town. The town wasn't built around an old rock quarry. The area wasn't bombed; nor was it struck by an enormous meteor.

What in the world could have created such a huge hole right in the middle of Winter Park?

It all began at about eight o'clock on the night of Friday, May 8, 1981, when the earth first started to move. The ground didn't shake the way it does in an earthquake. It just sank. Dust billowed up as the gritty limestone ground crumbled, creating a hole. The first spot to go was the front yard at 900 West Comstock Avenue. People gathered in amazement, watching as a huge sycamore tree dropped out of sight. The police quickly roped off the area, but they couldn't do anything to stop the earth from sinking.

By morning, the hole had expanded to about sixty feet in width and forty feet in depth and was still swallowing up everything in sight. Five Porsches and a camper parked at a car-repair lot slipped in. One whole house slid down, and so did parts of two more houses. Telephone lines had to be chopped free as telephone poles fell into the hole; water gushed from ruptured pipes, filling the bottom of the hole with muddy water.

Scientists knew the name of this hungry monster: a sinkhole. But neither they nor anyone else could

Most sinkholes are just small dips in the land, like Playa Lake in British Columbia.

Sometimes when a sinkhole forms, part of the cave roof doesn't collapse. This creates a natural bridge. You can see one if you visit Jefferson National Forest near Natural Bridge, Virginia.

stop it. By the time the Winter Park sinkhole finally stopped growing, two days after it first appeared, the hole was about four hundred feet wide and one hundred fifty feet across.

Sinkholes don't usually appear in the middle of a city. But they are common in any limestone area that normally gets a lot of rain. Kentucky, southern Indiana, and New Jersey, for example, have many sinkholes. But few are as large as the one in Winter Park. Most are just small dips in the land. The citizens of Winter Park considered hauling in dirt to fill the hole in the middle of their town. But they decided instead to turn it into a lake. In fact, that's what happens to many sinkholes: they fill with water.

A sinkhole starts out as a water-filled underground cavern in a limestone region. The water helps to support the weight of the cavern's ceiling and the soil above it. The city of Winter Park was built right over such a limestone cave— a very large one. There were no problems until a long dry spell dried out the whole area. People continued to use water, of course, even though no new rainwater soaked into the ground to replace what was drawn out. Gradually the cave was drained, and without the supporting water, the overlying surface layer finally cracked and collapsed.

THIS HOME IN ICELAND wasn't swallowed up by a sinkhole. But its owners surely didn't bury it themselves under all that black stuff. Is it mud? Or maybe the Icelanders' coal supply?

When Mount Saint Helens, in Washington, erupted on May 18, 1980,
winds spread volcanic ash as far away as Oklahoma and Minnesota.

Behind the house in the photograph you can see a mountain. This is no ordinary mountain, but a volcano. Before lava and ash began to explode into the air on January 3, 1973, there was only a flat plain where the volcanic mountain now stands. As the hot lava and ash began to rain down, people covered their roofs and windows with sheetmetal in an effort to protect their homes. Despite their efforts, twelve hundred homes—a third of the town of Vestmannaeyjar, which was closest to the volcano—

were destroyed. It's no wonder they named the new volcano Eldfell, "Fire Mountain." Within five months, the volcano had grown to a height of 705 feet.

A volcanic eruption, like a sinkhole, starts underground. Deep inside, the earth is so hot that solid rock melts. This molten rock, called magma, can remain underground and cool off and harden into new rocks. Or trapped gases may begin to build up pressure. Then the magma will rise to the surface through cracks in the

Sometimes the lava that explodes from a volcano is full of trapped gas. If the lava cools while the gas is still bubbling out, the rock that forms is full of holes. The stone sponge, called pumice, is often light enough to float on water.

Obsidian is volcanic glass. This rock, which is usually black, forms when lava cools very quickly.

earth's crust. And if overlying rock doesn't block it, the magma will ooze out onto the surface like toothpaste being squeezed out of a tube.

If the magma can't escape easily, though, the pressure builds up underground. Like soup boiling in a lidded pot, the pressure can eventually become great enough to cause an eruption. Then hot gas and magma suddenly explode into the air.

Magma that comes to the surface—whether gently or in a burst of energy—is called lava. When the lava cools and hardens, flows out again, and solidifies again, over and over, a volcanic mountain is formed. When some volcanoes erupt, lava simply oozes out. Others spew lava and ash thousands of feet into the air. When the lava contains so many gas bubbles that it's frothy like the foam on a glass of root beer, the tiny bits of molten rock material harden while they're still in the air. The ash that is formed can be blown many miles away by the wind. The house in Iceland is surrounded with ash that was blown several miles from the volcano.

Most changes in the earth come

Lava shrinks when it cools. That shrinking can cause cracking in the stone that forms. Sometimes those cracks go straight up through the lava flow, breaking it into pillars. People found it hard to believe that nature could create such regular pillars as these in Ireland, so they named this rock formation the Giants Causeway.

13

Devils Tower, in Wyoming, shows what can happen after a volcano dies out. What you see is the hard lava plug that was once the center of a volcano. All the rest of the cone-shaped mountain gradually eroded away.

about very slowly. But a volcanic eruption can drastically change the nearby area in a matter of hours or even minutes. Why would people choose to live within easy reach of a volcano? Most volcanoes are inactive, meaning that they have been known to erupt very rarely. Perhaps they have not been active for hundreds of years, so there isn't much danger. And minerals in volcanic ash make the soil very fertile, perfect for farming.

In Iceland, people even use the heat from the active volcanoes to heat their homes. To do this, water is piped through concrete-covered pipes, which absorb the earth's natural warmth. This form of energy is called geothermal energy. The water is then piped into buildings where the heat is radiated into the air, providing an inexpensive, pollution-free source of warmth. So, living near a volcano has its advantages.

15

THE BRAZILIAN PRINCESS topaz was cut from a stone discovered in Brazil. When the waterworn rock was found, it looked rough and dull. Luckily, an expert recognized the stone's potential beauty. But how did the gem cutter know what shape to cut the facets?

You've already seen some of the rock material that forms when magma cools and hardens above ground. If magma doesn't reach the surface, it still cools, eventually, but then the process happens much more slowly. If the magma is made up of minerals, a pure material, rather than a mixture of several kinds of materials, something special can occur.

When minerals have enough room within the surrounding rock to develop, they form crystals. The crystals for each type of mineral, including topaz, always have the same shape. Crystals take their shape from the orderly internal arrangement of their atoms, just as your body is shaped by your skeleton of bones.

If you look at some salt crystals

Even an uncut gemstone is a thing of beauty.

A bit of foreign material, which is known as an impurity, gives rubies their rich red color.

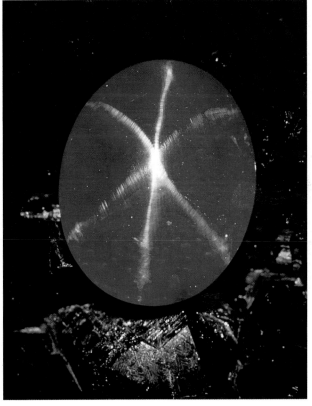

through a strong magnifying glass, you'll see that every grain of salt is a tiny cube. That's the shape of every salt crystal, no matter how small or large it is, because its atomic structure, its "skeleton," is in the form of a cube. Likewise, topaz crystals are always ortho-rhombic (or-tho-RAHM-bic). Or-

thorhombic crystals have three unequal sides that form right angles where the sides meet.

Gemstones are created from raw crystals by polishing and cutting especially durable crystals. Gem cutters must work with the natural atomic pattern within the crystal to avoid splitting or fracturing the

Emerald gemstones are rarely perfect. Most contain tiny fractures, because emerald is a very brittle crystal and cracks quite easily.

Most large topazes are pale blue or colorless. Because pink ones are the rarest, and therefore the most valuable, people sometimes heat yellow topaz to turn it pink.

stone, which, although durable, is often brittle. That's why gemstones are cut only into certain characteristic designs.

Before any facets are cut, a stone is roughly shaped and then polished in a revolving drum, where it is tumbled with water and a coarse grinding grit to smooth the surfaces. The process is repeated several times, tumbling the crystal with water and increasingly finer grits. The last tumbling is done with a polishing powder to give the gem its sparkle. Only then does the gem cutter carefully cut facets onto the stone's surface.

Polishing and cutting the Brazilian Princess took more than two years. The crystal from which it was cut weighed an amazing twenty-six pounds; the finished gem is as large as an automobile headlight and weighs about ten pounds. Still, it is only the second-largest gemstone in the world. The Champagne topaz weighs over sixteen pounds!

Crystals are used for more than gemstones, though. They are much more valuable for use in industry: in dentists' drills, hearing aids, and communications equipment, for example. Most diamonds are used as cutting and grinding tools. Diamond is the hardest known mineral—only another diamond can scratch it. You may have a diamond or ruby nail file at home.

And you probably use the most common crystal every day—to flavor your food. Would you like to taste a crystal? Just put a pinch of salt on your tongue! Salt is one crystal that is basic to the diet and health of every animal on earth.

CRYSTALS aren't the only amazing shapes that mineral deposits form. Just look at this spectacular display at Minerva Terrace in Yellowstone National Park. At first glance, you might think you are looking at a frozen waterfall. But what you see isn't water at all.

What looks like a *water*fall at Minerva Terrace is actually a *mineral* fall. Pools of molten magma heat up water that collects deep underground until it's superhot. Because the water is under pressure, its temperature can be well above the normal boiling point without turning the water to steam. Eventually, natural convection currents that make liquids circulate cause the hot water to rise.

Then the rising water absorbs volcanic gases, especially carbon dioxide, so that it becomes a weak kind of carbonic acid. As this acidic water passes through a thick layer of limestone, it dissolves some of the rock and then carries the limestone material to the surface. There, the carbon dioxide gas escapes into the air, the hot water evaporates or trickles away, and the dissolved limestone is left behind as a mineral deposit called travertine. This creates the fanciful mineral deposits.

Minerva Terrace grows and changes nearly as rapidly as an actual waterfall. A layer of travertine about a foot thick is deposited every year. Nearly two tons of travertine are deposited daily throughout the hot-spring terraces in Yellowstone National Park.

Yellowstone National Park is a treasure trove of natural wonders, where you can actually see the earth changing. In several places escaping steam and gas boil up through mud flats, creating bubbling ponds and puddles.

Yellowstone also has many geysers: places where steam and water shoot high into the air from deep underground. The water doesn't merely seep, or even pour, out of a geyser. It comes spouting skyward in a hot, roaring, powerful jet.

The geyser is created by cool water seeping into a rock chamber deep underground. The rock in some areas of Yellowstone is so porous that it is estimated that the water soaking into the ground quickly percolates down to depths of ten thousand feet or more. At such depths, the heat from surrounding magma turns this water superhot. So, when natural currents cause the water to begin to rise and the pressure on it is reduced, some of the water becomes steam. The result is something like popcorn popping. The greater volume of the exploding steam pushes water in the rock "pipe" above it high into the air in its rush to escape from the chamber.

The downward movement of water through the earth can create spectacular effects, too. In limestone caves, such as Carlsbad Caverns in New Mexico, you can find formations that will remind you of Minerva Falls. Because limestone is so porous and has many cracks, or

Old Faithful is probably the best-known geyser—and the most regular. About once every hour, as much as 12,000 gallons of boiling water and steam spurt more than 200 feet into the air.

People sometimes have trouble remembering which formations, such as these at Carlsbad Caverns, are stalagmites and which are stalactites, until they realize that stalactites hang on **tight** to the **c**eiling and stalag**m**ites **might** make it to the top from the **g**round.

fissures, water can soak through it easily. Over many, many years, the water dissolves the limestone and carries it away, making the cracks larger and larger. Eventually, they may become large enough to be called caves.

The mineral water passing through the stone forms droplets when it reaches the ceiling of a cave. Sometimes the water evaporates before it drips to the floor. The minerals it carried are left on the ceiling in a film along the outer edge of the droplet. The next drop deposits its film on the first, and so

on. Icicle-shaped rocks are gradually formed. If the water drips to the cave floor and then evaporates, the minerals that are left form pillars. Sometimes the icicles and pillars keep growing for so long— thousands of years—that they meet and form columns from floor to ceiling.

It takes hundreds of years for stalactites (icicles) and stalagmites (pillars) to grow only an inch. Some stretch more than a hundred feet in length. Imagine how long it must have taken for those giants to form!

MINERAL RESIDUES aren't the only deposits that shape the earth's surface. Snow and ice can build up into a huge body of ice. You may not be surprised to read that glaciers, like this one on Mount Spurr, Alaska, are hundreds of feet across, several thousand feet thick, and many miles long. But did you know that glaciers travel?

The movement of glacial ice is due mainly to the glacier's own massive weight. Usually, ice must be warmed to a temperature above 32°F before it will melt. If ice is under pressure, however, it will melt at a lower temperature. Imagine how heavy a huge glacier is! The sheer pressure of the overlying layers of ice is enough to melt the ice at the bottom of the glacier, helping it move over the ground.

Glaciers form when snow piles up, layer upon layer, in mountain hollows. As the snow gets deeper and deeper, its own weight packs it into ice. Then as more snow and ice are added to the formation, the glacier spills over and begins to flow downhill.

Glaciers don't all move at the same rate, though. Some move only a few feet per year; others, several yards per day. Still others have periods of rapid movement, called surges, followed by periods when they don't move at all. No one is quite sure why these glaciers have sporadic movement. One idea of what happens is that the ice may become frozen tight to the bedrock underneath it—the way a

As glaciers age and travel, they pick up stones and dirt. Their surfaces are not smooth and even, but more like thick shards of glass.

wet hand sticks to cold metal; then sudden melting releases the glacier.

Parts of a single glacier also move at different speeds. Friction, from dragging over the bedrock, slightly slows the movement of the ice at the bottom of the glacier. Likewise, if the glacier is traveling through a mountain valley, it drags along the walls, which slows the flow along the sides. So the center of the glacier moves the fastest. By putting stakes in glacial ice and measuring movement, scientists have proved that a glacier is not a truly solid block of ice and that the center really does advance the fastest.

Whenever a glacier travels, even if it moves only a few inches, it changes the surface of the earth. Glaciers "pluck" rocks from the ground beneath them, dragging them many miles from their original location. This scouring action also scrapes the surface of the earth as if the glacier's bottom were lined with sandpaper. In addition, glaciers carry with them rocks and other materials that fall onto their surfaces.

Glaciers don't only remove stone; they leave some behind as

Glaciers sometimes form on several sides of a mountain at once. Each glacier carves away some rock, especially near the peak. That's how the Matterhorn, in Switzerland, got such an unusually pointed peak.

Yosemite National Park's Half Dome was created by the shearing action of glacial movement.

well. If weather conditions warm up or if the glacier reaches a region where the climate is warmer, the ice begins to melt. When the rate at which the ice is melting equals the rate of its advance, the glacier drops its load. The result is likely to be a large boulder sitting in the middle of an otherwise unrocky field. Or it may be an oddly unsorted mixture of large stones and smaller rock fragments. Such a mixture is called till.

Today, the biggest sheets of ice exist in Greenland and Antarctica. At several times in the past, though, ice covered large parts of the earth's surface. In North America, ice spread from the North Pole to Ohio, Indiana, and North Carolina. These periods of cold and ice, which lasted many thousands of years, are known as the ice ages.

As these massive ice sheets melted in periods of warmer weather, meltwater flowed out and formed new rivers. Rock and ice that were dropped by the melting glaciers dammed existing rivers, forming lakes. More lakes were created when blocks of ice broke off and slowly melted. Many of Minnesota's "ten thousand lakes," as well as the Great Lakes, were created when the huge ice-age glaciers melted.

WATER can move rocks many miles. But this traveling stone and its track are in the dry desert of Death Valley, California. Some such stones weigh 500 pounds and have left tracks 280 yards long. This stone was not propelled by water or ice—what could have moved it?

In regions with wide-open spaces, dunes may form a series of long ridges. Dunes are far-from-permanent structures—they migrate and change shape every time the wind blows.

Do you think you could move a 500-pound boulder by blowing on it? Or even a rock the size of your fist? No? Maybe a grain of sand?

In a flat, level area such as Death Valley, the strength of winds during a storm is as great as the force of your breath blowing a grain of sand. But these large rocks don't usually get moved by dry-weather winds. That is because even though the land is flat, hard-packed earth and there are no plants in the way,

the dry desert floor isn't as smooth as it might seem to be. During a heavy rainstorm, however, the surface layer turns into slick mud. Then, when strong winds give the stones a push, away they go, leaving their trails behind them as evidence of their travels.

Under the right conditions, strong winds can move large boulders. They can and do lift sand and carry it away far more easily. When the winds slow down, the sand

Windblown sand scours the rocks on the earth's surface, blasting off small chips of stone and even smaller particles. Even strong winds don't lift the sand very high, though. "Sandblasting" and weathering created a number of rock arches, like this one in Arches National Park in Utah.

drops to the ground and piles up in dunes. As the dunes grow higher, a gentle slope forms on the side from which the winds most often blow. The sand on the side away from the wind becomes unstable, though; there, it slides down from the top, forming a steep slope. So, gradually, the dune is shaped into a graceful crescent.

Particles of topsoil, especially dry ones, can be blown away by winds even more easily than sand. This is because dry soil weighs less than sand. The lighter weight also enables the wind to carry soil much higher and farther than it can carry sand.

Between 1933 and 1939, unusually dry weather combined with

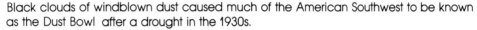

Black clouds of windblown dust caused much of the American Southwest to be known as the Dust Bowl after a drought in the 1930s.

poor farming practices left large areas of soil in the American Southwest without sufficient plant cover to protect it and hold it down. Strong winds carried thousands of pounds of the dry topsoil high into the sky. When the winds slowed or shifted, these "black blizzards" heaped dust into huge drifts all through the area. The long-lasting drought and high winds eventually turned fifty million acres of once-fertile land in Texas, New Mexico, Colorado, Kansas, and Oklahoma into deserts of blowing dust.

The federally funded Conservation Reserve Program has paid farmers in the devastated Dust Bowl region to plant some of their land in permanent grass in order to anchor the topsoil once again. The fine, intertwining roots of grasses hold the soil in place better than other plants can.

YOU'VE SEEN how ice and wind can move anything from dust to boulders. Now look at this picture of a house on a lake in Sea Breeze, New York. The owners originally built the house on top of the hill. Why did they move it into the lake?

If you have ever played at the edge of a lake where waves were lapping the shore, you've felt the gentle tug of the water as it flows off the beach and back into the lake. You may have felt this tug even more strongly if you've visited the ocean and played in the surf. You probably also noticed that the water washes sand and pebbles and sometimes shells onto the shore when the waves come in and pulls some of them back when the waves go back out. The movement of water along a shoreline never stops. This action transports sand and pebbles along the shore. And the constant washing in and out also wears away, or erodes, the shoreline.

That's what happened to the house in Sea Breeze. The water washed away enough soil to undercut the base of the hillside on which the house was built. Eventually this so weakened the hill that the soil above collapsed, carrying the house down with it into the lake.

If small waves along a quiet lakeshore can move the earth beneath them, think what force smashing ocean waves pack—and how much they can alter the shape of shores and cliffs. Of course, waves don't move a whole rocky cliff at once. Just as the New York lakeside hill was reshaped a little at a time, ocean waves gradually wear away a cliff's base. Then overhanging rocks from the top fall into the sea. On Martha's Vineyard, an island off the coast of Massachusetts, about five feet of the cliff is being worn away every year. Imagine how normal coastal weathering is speeded up when a hurricane smashes even more powerful waves against the shore!

Rivers are powerful land movers too, especially in spring and early summer when the flowing waters are high and swift. Like glaciers, rivers can tear pieces of rock of all sizes away from their banks and off their riverbeds. Then as this rock debris is carried along, the pebbles and boulders bump against the banks, jarring even more soil and rock loose to be carried away.

The Colorado River has been carving away at the Grand Canyon for millions of years, and it's still going strong. The shape of the canyon walls varies because of the differences in the rock layers. Soft layers erode faster than harder ones.

Where does the soil and stone carried by rivers end up? If there's

You can clearly see the notch cut by waves at high tide on the coast of Sonora, Mexico.

The Colorado River hauls as much as 500,000 tons of soil, rock, and sand out of the Grand Canyon every day. That's enough to fill two million quarter-ton pickup trucks!

a flood, the river spreads some of this material onto land. The sediment, or fine particles of soil, makes the land richer and more fertile. In ancient Egypt, people depended on the regular flooding of the Nile River to bring fresh soil to their farms. Today, because the Aswan High Dam controls the floodwaters, farmers must use fertilizers to enrich the soil instead of receiving a fresh coating of naturally fertile soil for their fields. During dry periods, however, water is also available for irrigation.

Waves at Cape Kiwanda, Oregon, never stop working away at the shoreline cliffs.

Wherever it's possible, rivers flow toward the sea. So, much of the material they carry ends up in the ocean. The Red, Missouri, and Mississippi rivers connect. At the mouth of the Mississippi in the Gulf of Mexico, the flow of water slows down as it moves into the gulf, and its load of rock and soil drops to the bottom.

Over many years, silting action has built up a large fan-shaped area of land, known as the Mississippi Delta, at the mouth of the river.

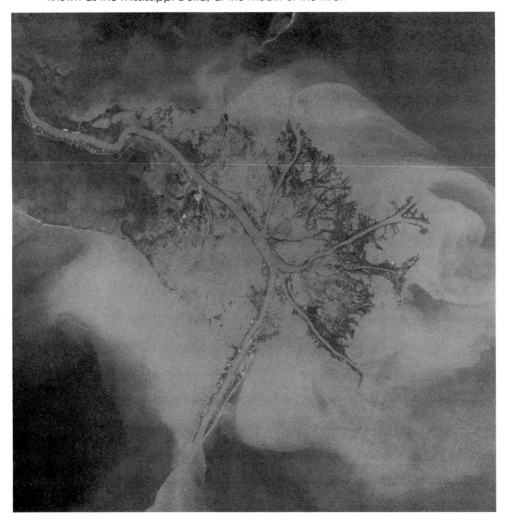

NOW YOU KNOW SOME OF THE WAYS in which the earth you live on is constantly changing. Water and wind action on the surface and heat deep underground are at work eroding and rebuilding and re-shaping the earth even as you read this. So the next time you're notic-ing what's going on in your neigh-borhood, take a close look at the earth too.

The earth is alive with constant activity. And that makes it a fasci-nating place to live!

INDEX